peak light

Parkhouse Hill and Chrome Hill from Glutton Bridge

the peak district photography of

THANKS

First and foremost, thanks go to my wife, Jan, without whose help and encouragement this book would have been more stressful and taken considerably longer to produce.

Thanks also to:

Roger Maile for his advice and hard work in calmly pulling together all the elements to produce *Peak Light* in an amazingly short timescale;

Andy Oakley for his design work;

Steven Brierley and his colleagues at Harman Technology Ltd (Ilford Photo) and Keith Sanderson of Johnsons Photopia (Mamiya UK) for their support;

Christine Johnson and Peter Kersh, of UK Trade and Investment, for encouragement and financial support to push my business forward;

Design Factory for financial support and encouragement;

Members of Peak District Products and High Peak Artists and Craftworkers Association, especially to Pauline Townsend, for encouragement and help over the last two years;

and finally, thanks to all the people who have purchased photographs and attended my courses and to those who bought my first book, *High Light*, in such quantities that it sold out and was reprinted within two years.

PRINTS AND FURTHER INFORMATION

Prints and further information are available from my business website:
www.davebutcher.net

PEAK LIGHT
Dave Butcher

Published in the UK by Dave Butcher Photography
Briarwood, Tunstead Milton, Whaley Bridge, High Peak, Derbyshire, SK23 7ER
www.davebutcher.net

© Dave Butcher Photography, 2007
The images and text in this book are the copyright of Dave Butcher who asserts his moral rights to be identified as the author of the work. Copyright, 2007.

British Library Cataloguing-in-Publication Data:
A catalogue record for the book is available from the British Library.

ISBN 978-0-9555627-0-9
First edition, 2007

Design and editorial production by Roger Maile Consultancy
20 St Peters Road, Croydon, CR0 1HD
Printed in England by Gemini Press Ltd.

introduction: the Peak District

The Peak District stretches from near Ashbourne in the South to near Holmfirth in the north, a distance of about 50 miles, and from Macclesfield in the West to Chesterfield in the East, about 30 miles.

Created in 1951, it was the first National Park in the UK and is, allegedly, the second most visited National Park in the world after Yellowstone in the USA – the reason for this being that it is surrounded by large towns and cities.

There are no soaring peaks like those in the Lake District, Snowdonia or the Scottish Highlands, but this is more than compensated by the varied countryside.

There are two distinct areas called White Peak (after the limestone dales in the south) and Dark Peak (peat bog country in the north and west) – and they are very different in character.

The Limestone dales are often steep-sided gorges, enclosing a fast running river or stream, with the odd peak, spire, cave and arch, often linked by wider areas of farmland and grazing. Between the dales is rolling grassy farmland divided by the ubiquitous dry stone walls with small copses of trees breaking the skyline at intervals. Dove Dale is probably the most famous of all of the Derbyshire Dales, but is just 2 or 3 miles of the 45 miles' length of the River Dove, from its source on Axe Edge near Buxton. Each short section of Dale that it runs through has a different name.

Peat bog country, on the other hand, is more rolling, covered in brown peat, heather and tussocky grasses. The purple heather looks fantastic in late August in the sunshine. Once again, there are dry stone walls everywhere and streams and rivers that run pretty reliably, as might be expected in an area that receives up to 2 metres of rainfall a year.

The highest areas are here too, with the summit of Kinderscout at 636m (2087 ft) being the highest point in Derbyshire, although I use 'summit' in the broadest sense of the word: it really is not obvious when you reach the top of this immense peat bog area. This is also the location of the highest waterfall in Derbyshire, Kinder Downfall at 30m (100 ft). This dries up in the summer as the River Kinder is absorbed by the peat before it reaches the falls.

Peak Light is roughly arranged geographically from south to north. The position of each location is shown on the map on page 4 and this, together with the caption for each picture, will help you to follow in my footsteps.

The photographs concentrate on the landscapes rather than the many villages and even with this focus, space limitations may mean I have still omitted some places that you would have liked to be included.

Since 1988, I have lived in the small village of Tunstead Milton, between Whaley Bridge and Chapel-en-le-Frith, towards the north of the Peak District. The immediate area is great for solitary walking since it is not as visited as some in the Peaks, although the scenery is just as spectacular to my eyes.

I hope these images of the Peak District will inspire you, as much as it does me, to visit and enjoy the area in all of its varied seasons.

image locations

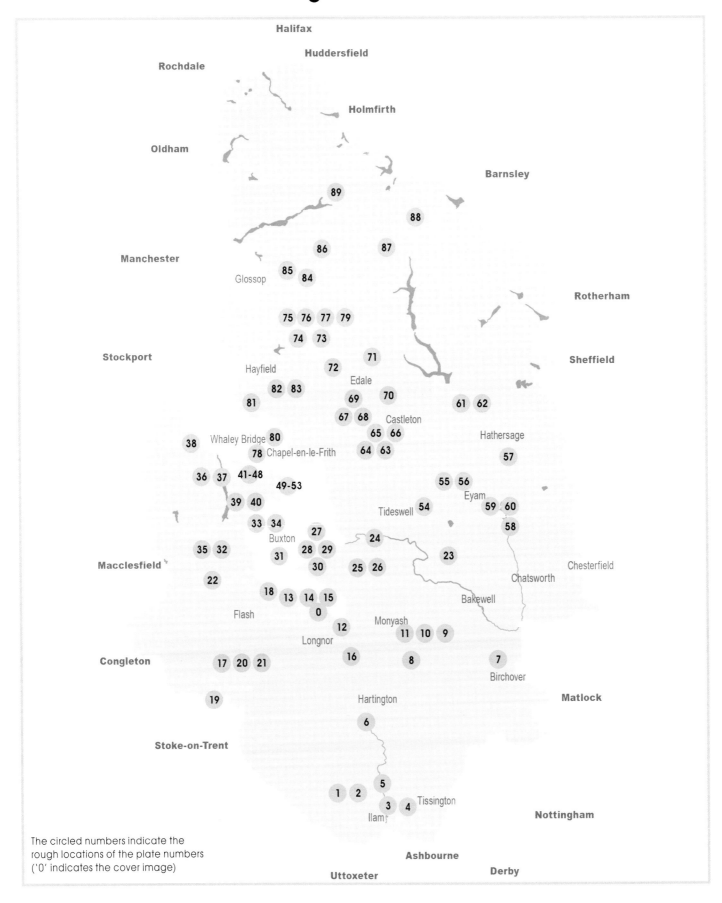

Halifax

Huddersfield

Rochdale

Holmfirth

Oldham

Barnsley

Manchester

89

88

86

87

Glossop

85 84

Rotherham

75 76 77 79

74 73

Stockport

Sheffield

71

72

Hayfield

Edale

82 83

69 70

81

67 68

Castleton

65 66

Hathersage

Whaley Bridge 80

64 63

61 62

38

78 Chapel-en-le-Frith

57

36 37 41-48

55 56

49-53

Eyam

39 40

Tideswell 54

59 60

33 34

58

27

Buxton

24

35 32

28 29

23

31

30

25 26

Chesterfield

22

Chatsworth

18 13 14 15

Bakewell

Flash

0

12

Monyash

Longnor

11 10 9

16

8

Congleton

17 20 21

7

Birchover

19

Hartington

Matlock

6

Stoke-on-Trent

5

1 2

3 4 Tissington

Ilam

Nottingham

The circled numbers indicate the
rough locations of the plate numbers
('0' indicates the cover image)

Ashbourne

Derby

Uttoxeter

(top) **1 – Above the Manifold Valley**
(bottom) **2 – Wetton Hill and beyond**
Plates 1 and 2 from Mere Hill, north of Calton

(top left) **3 – Trees and fields from Thorpe Cloud**
(bottom left) **4 – Thorpe Cloud shadow and Dovedale**
Plates 3 and 4 from the summit of Thorpe Cloud

(above) **5 – Dovedale torrent**
A few hundred yards upstream from the famous Stepping Stones

(above) **6 – River Dove and Wolfscote Dale**
From the Hartington end of the dale

(top right) **7 – Nine Ladies stone circle, Stanton Moor**
(bottom right) **8 – Arbor Low stone circle**

(top left) **9 – Lathkill Falls**
(bottom left) **10 – Lathkill Dale rocks and trees**
(above) **11 – Lathkill Head cave and River Lathkill**
The river flows out of the cave entrance in all but the driest of weather

Plates 9-11 taken at the Monyash end of the dale.

12 – High Wheeldon summit view towards Chrome Hill (in background shadow on the left)

13 – Chrome Hill taken from the summit of Parkhouse Hill

(above) **14 – Chrome Hill taken from the rock pillar (Sugarloaf) above the Dowel Dale road**

(top right) **15 – Parkhouse Hill summit (left) with Chrome Hill in the background**

(bottom right) **16 – Chrome Hill and Parkhouse Hill**
From Pilsbury Castle, between Longnor and Hartington

(*above*)   **17 – Hen Cloud from the Roaches, summer**

(*top right*)   **18 – Parkhouse Hill from the lower slopes of Chrome Hill**

(*bottom right*)   **19 – The Roaches (left) and Hen Cloud (right) and spring meadow**

(left) **20 – The Roaches western edge with Hen Cloud in the background**

(above) **21 – Hen Cloud from The Roaches, winter**

(top left) **22 – Three Shires Head Falls near Flash**
(bottom left) **23 – Monsal Dale from Monsal Head**
(above) **24 – Chee Dale stepping stones**
The section nearest to Buxton

25 – Chelmorton snowy hills
From Chelmorton Low

26 – Chelmorton Fields
Taken from the lower slopes of Chelmorton Low

27 – Deep Dale, summer

28 – Deep Dale, winter
Plates 27 and 28 taken from the footpath between King Sterndale and Chelmorton

29 – Tree shadows

30 – Trees in winter
Plates 29 and 30 taken between King Sterndale and Cowdale

31 – Solomon's Temple, Buxton
This tower is on Grin Low to the south of Buxton

32 – Goyt Valley Falls
These are below the road near the old packhorse bridge beyond Errwood Hall

33 – Snowy treetops, Buxton

34 – Snowy trees #1, Buxton
Plates 33 and 34 are beside the road to Whaley Bridge

35 – Shutlingsloe from the summit of Shining Tor

36 – Shining Tor (background left) from Windgather Rocks, near Kettleshulme

(left) **37 – Windgather Rocks sky**
(above) **38 – Windgather Rocks (background right)**
From Bailey's Farm, near Whaley Bridge

(top left) **39 – Goyt Valley and Taxal Edge, summer**
(bottom left) **40 – Goyt Valley and Taxal Edge, winter**
Plates 39-40 were taken from above Long Hill: the walls were recently rebuilt, so the view has changed!

(above) **41 – Snowboarder near Combs**
With Castle Naze in the background

(above) **42 – Lone tree #1, winter**
(top right) **43 – Lone tree #2, winter and clouds**
(right: bottom left) **44 – Lone tree #3, infrared**
(right: bottom right) **45 – Lone tree #4, mist**
Plates 42-45 were taken at Ladder Hill, Goyt Valley, near Whaley Bridge

(top left) **46 – Beech tree, Ladder Hill, Goyt Valley, near Whaley Bridge**
(bottom left) **47 – Combs Moss from Thorny Lee above the village of Combs**
(above) **48 – Combs Reservoir reflection from the dam, Tunstead Milton**

49 – White Peak in winter
Pyegreave Farm from Combs Moss

50 – Tree and stream, near Combs

51 – Woodland in autumn #1, near Combs

52 – Woodland in autumn #2, near Combs

53 – Old tree, near Combs
Plates 50-53 are on private land

54 – Peter Stone near Litton
Taken from the Wardlow Mires side

55 – Waterfall Swallet #1

56 – Waterfall Swallet #2
Plates 55 and 56: The second highest waterfall in Derbyshire, allegedly, sits
in a deep hollow near the road between Foolow and Eyam

57 – Bole Hill millstones
In the old quarry on the hill behind Grindleford Station

58 – Curbar Edge millstone, storm
Above the village of Curbar; an electrical storm in the background

(top) **59 – Frogatt Edge from the Curbar Edge side**
(bottom) **60 – Tree on Frogatt Edge**

(top) **61 – Bamford Edge view towards Bradwell**
(bottom) **62 – Ladybower Reservoir from Bamford Edge**

63 – Castleton from Winnat's Pass

64 – Win Hill and Castleton from Winnat's Pass
Plates 63 and 64 were taken from the rim accessed from the road at the top of the pass

65 – Winnat's Pass crags
Taken from the opposite side of the pass to plates 63-64

66 – Mam Tor from near the top of Winnat's Pass

(above) **67 – Mam Tor from Rushup Edge**
(top right) **68 – Tree and Mam Tor, Rushup Edge**
(bottom right) **69 – Lose Hill from Mam Tor summit**

70 – Back Tor, between Mam Tor and Lose Hill

71 – Win Hill (left) and Lose Hill (right) from the south edge of Kinderscout

72 – Clouds in the valley, near Crowden Brook, Kinderscout

73 – Hare tracks in snow, near Kinder Low

(top left) **74 – Kinder Low, Kinderscout**
(bottom left) **75 – Kinder Downfall, icy**
(above) **76 – Kinder Downfall, snowy**

(top left)   77 – Kinder Downfall, windy day
(bottom left)   78 – Kinderscout from Eccles Pike #1, near Tunstead Milton
(above)   79 – Kinder Downfall in full flow

(left) **80 – Kinderscout from Eccles Pike #3, near Tunstead Milton**
(above) **81 – Kinderscout from Cracken Edge, near Chinley**

82 – Kinderscout from Mount Famine, near Hayfield, summer

83 – Kinderscout from Mount Famine, near Hayfield, winter

84 – Doctors Gate, Bleaklow #1, near Glossop

85 – Doctors Gate, Bleaklow #2, near Glossop

(left) **86 – 'The Kiss', the Wainstones, at Bleaklow Head (633m)**
(above) **87 – Grinah Stones, Upper Derwent Valley, with Bleaklow in the background**

88 – Crow Stones Edge, north of Howden Reservoir

89 – Black Clough waterfall
On the north edge of Bleaklow near the Woodhead pass

photography notes

When working in the Peak District I apply the same principles that I use for landscape photography anywhere: first find the viewpoint and then take the picture when the weather is right for what I want to achieve. Wandering around aimlessly in the hope that something will turn up can work, but is not a very reliable technique!

Research is important for new areas, so visiting on more than one occasion gives a better appreciation of what is possible. Then, when conditions are right, I can go and take the shot I want and not waste time looking for the best positions since I already know them.

I have exclusively used Mamiya medium format cameras since 1993 and used them extensively for several years before this. Mostly I used Mamiya 6 cameras (12 negatives per roll of 120 film) but in 2006 I switched to Mamiya 7 (10 negatives per film). This gave me rectangular negatives (6 x 7 cm), instead of the square negatives (6 x 6 cm) I had become used to, and more lenses to choose from (6 instead of 3). The cameras are very similar in dimensions, weight and ease of use, so the change was quite easy to make. The only difficulty I had was in remembering to rotate the camera for vertical shots, something I had not needed to do in the 13 years of using the Mamiya 6.

My cameras are rangefinder-type, which means that I compose through a small window in the top left corner (as viewed from behind) of the camera and not through the lens. Each lens has its own shutter, resulting in a camera that is lighter and smaller than would otherwise be the case.

I am careful when composing a shot to look around the edges of the viewfinder and not just in the centre. Moving camera position and height to put something in the right position relative to something else in the shot is really important. The camera is always on a lightweight tripod too so that this can be controlled more easily. My tripods are always fitted with quick release heads. The landscape is continually changing, especially in the Peak District, and often the light will be gone if I don't work fast.

Placing subjects centrally works for symmetrical images but for pretty much everything else placing the key subjects and picture elements well off-centre, horizontally and vertically, works best for me. Lines that lead in from the edge of the shot are often used as strong picture elements, as are objects in the foreground, such as boulders, trees, etc. I don't like any important picture element to cut the skyline unless it is really important that it does so, in which case it is done in an obvious way to emphasise it.

I like to have everything in focus from front to back in the picture. The easiest way to do this is to use a wide angle lens: they focus closer than other lenses. My favourite for both Mamiya 6 and Mamiya 7 is the 50 mm. The Mamiya 7 also has a 43 mm lens which can give some great shots in tight situations although I use this with caution since it can make anything in the background appear quite small.

The other pre-requisite is the use of a small aperture, often the f/22 limit of the lens. Using something called hyperfocal distance instead of always focussing on infinity adds a little bit of extra scope for closer focussing. This is easy on the Mamiya cameras since it just requires that the focussing line on the lens is rotated back from the infinity line to the f/stop set on the lens. In fact, for optimum results, I generally use a point two stops less than the f/stop in use. For example, this means the focus line is turned to f/11 when using f/22. This also means that I very seldom need to focus the cameras using the split screen focussing system in the camera's built-in viewfinder, excellent though it is.

In the past I generally used the meter on the camera for determining exposure. However, in the last few years I have used a Sekonic spot meter for most of my work. This is more reliable and lets me check the light reading for all important areas of the image before I decide what camera settings I want. The old adage for black and white film, which still works today, is 'expose for the shadows'. For Ilford FP4 Plus 120, the film that I use almost exclusively, very little detail will be recorded beyond 3 stops of underexposure, so that limitation also guides the exposure setting. Finally, bracketing 1 stop under and over in cases of uncertainty ensures that a good negative will be obtained from almost any lighting situation.

photography notes

Filters are important for good black and white results and I always use the screw-on variety to avoid blocking the rangefinder focussing system. The colours that I use are:
- Green to lighten green foliage to light grey;
- Yellow to darken blue skies without darkening shadows and green leaves too much;
- Orange to darken blue skies to dark grey (this can darken green leaves and shadows too much, so I use with caution), and
- Dark Yellow as a compromise between Orange and Yellow. (Prints made from Dark Yellow filtered negatives are invariably easier to print than those made using an Orange filter but may need more exposure of the sky than would be the case had an Orange filter been used.)

Infrared shots convert blue skies into dark grey while at the same time changing green deciduous foliage, grasses and bracken into shades of light grey. Coniferous trees do not usually give off much infrared and so remain dark grey in infrared images. I use Ilford SFX infrared film, relaunched in 2007 (using my images on the Ilford promotional material) after an absence of two years, to achieve interesting effects from the infrared effect while retaining a realistic look to the landscape. I don't like the more extreme, almost surreal, effects that some infrared films can give. The SFX film must be used with a special filter such as that from Ilford or the Heliopan 715 that I use.

I have tried lots of different carrying systems for my camera gear over the years. The one that has proved the most convenient and comfortable is to carry the camera on the front just above my waist, using a shoulder harness. The case opens at the top and either takes one camera or two. Mostly I use two cameras, both loaded with Ilford FP4 Plus, one with the 50mm lens, the other either with the 150mm or 43mm lens. The third lens is carried in a small lens case clipped to the camera case. For exposed film, I use a little case with an elasticated top section such that I can push films into this through the seal and know they will not be able to fall or jump out.

I usually carry a normal mountain rucsac for my hill gear of between 35 litres and 50 litres capacity. My small, lightweight tripod hangs from a karabiner threaded through the rucsac shoulder strap with the legs held by another karabiner or strap to the hip belt of the rucsac. Everything is immediately to hand; there is no need to stop and take the rucsac off my back to get at any camera gear before taking pictures. I use the same system for all of my landscape work, whether I am walking, hiking, mountaineering or skiing.

I do not use the zone system as invented by Ansel Adams: I never change my development for individual negatives. I have found this unnecessary for my work with modern photographic printing papers like the Ilford Multigrade range and techniques like split grade printing. All of my films are processed in Ilford Ilfotec DDX developer diluted 1+6 (a liquid concentrate that gives results similar to the powder developer ID11).

When it comes to making the print, I use split grade printing for everything. In fact every print in this book is a split grade print. All that this means is that I split the main exposure into two and use a combination of a low contrast and a high contrast exposure. I generally use grade 0 to 1.5 for the low contrast exposure and grade 5 for the high contrast exposure. With my negatives, it usually works out that an exposure ratio of 1:2 is about right or at least a good starting point.

I use a very simple logic in working out the grade and times for each of the two basic exposures. The highlight detail mainly comes from the low contrast exposure so if I need more detail, I increase this or reduce the grade towards towards zero. The blacks in my prints come mainly from the high contrast exposure so I adjust this as each negative requires to give detail in the shadows. There is also one extra option that specifically helps shadow details: dodging (reducing) the shadows during the low contrast exposure. What this does is effectively reduce or remove the low contrast exposure from the shadows which separates the tones here enormously and gives real punch to the darker print areas. I often use this same technique for the foreground to add 'punch' to the bottom of the print, since this is what everything else sits on!

If you would like to know more about me and my photography, to buy original photographs or see details of courses that I run, please look at my web site: www.davebutcher.net